MW01251020

ISAT Test Practice for Reading and Writing

Grade 1

Harcourt School Publishers

www.harcourtschool.com

Printed in the United States of America

ISBN 10: 0-15-374489-8
ISBN 13: 978-0-15-374489-1

1 2 3 4 5 6 7 8 9 10   862   16 15 14 13 12 11 10 09 08 07

Contents

Short passage (Fiction)

Listen to the story "School for Lucky." Then answer Numbers 1 through 3.

School for Lucky

May's puppy Lucky wanted to go to school with May.

"No dogs in school," May had said.

All day, Lucky waited for May by the door. At last, May came home! Lucky wagged his tail.

"I think Lucky wants to go to school," said May's mom. "I have an idea."

The next day May's mom, Lucky, and May went to a pet store.

Inside the store was a classroom for pets. A teacher showed May how to make Lucky speak, lie down, and sit. Finally, the teacher gave May a book about dog tricks. Lucky got a bone!

GO ON ▶

1

In the beginning,
Lucky wanted to —

Ⓐ wag his tail
Ⓑ go to school with
   May
Ⓒ get a bone

3

What happened at the
end of the story?

Ⓐ Lucky stayed home.
Ⓑ Lucky waited by
   the door.
Ⓒ Lucky got a bone!

2

In the pet classroom,
the teacher showed
May how to —

Ⓐ make Lucky sit
Ⓑ make Lucky read
Ⓒ play with other dogs

GO ON ▶

Short passage (Fiction)

Teacher Read-Aloud

Listen to the story "A Musical Family." Then answer Numbers 4 through 6.

A Musical Family

Alex loves music. Alex has two brothers. They love music, too. Both of Alex's brothers play an instrument. His oldest brother, Jay, plays the drums. His younger brother, David, plays the horn. Jay and David like to play their instruments together. They think Alex should learn to play an instrument, too.

"It would be fun to play together," Jay tells Alex.

Alex thinks about it. He loves music. It could be fun to play an instrument. But what Alex really loves is singing. He tells his brothers he wants to sing.

"You can sing while we play," Jay says.

"That sounds like a great idea," David adds.

GO ON ▶

4

How is Alex different from his brothers?

Ⓐ Alex wants to sing.

Ⓑ Alex wanted to play the drums.

Ⓒ Alex does not like music.

5

What do Jay and David like to do?

Ⓐ They both like to sing.

Ⓑ They both play horns.

Ⓒ They like to play together.

6

How does this story end?

Ⓐ Alex sings and his brothers play instruments.

Ⓑ Jay learned to sing.

Ⓒ David and Alex both play the drums.

GO ON ▶

Short passage (Fiction)

Listen to the story "The New Girl." Then answer Numbers 7 through 11.

The New Girl

One day a new girl <u>joined</u> Tamika's class. The new girl's name was Marta. She had moved from Texas. Marta didn't have any friends at her new school.

At lunch time Tamika asked Marta to sit with her. The girls ate lunch together. They laughed and talked. They played together on the playground. They went on the slide and played in the sand.

Tamika said, "This is your school now. You should know your way around." Tamika showed Marta the school.

Marta said, "When I came to school today, I was scared. I didn't know anyone. Now I have a friend and a nice new school!"

GO ON ▶

7 What is another way to say <u>joined</u>?

Ⓐ came to
Ⓑ left
Ⓒ met

10 What is another good title for this story?

Ⓐ Making a Friend
Ⓑ The Art Room
Ⓒ The Kind Teacher

8 Where does this story take place?

Ⓐ in Texas
Ⓑ in a school
Ⓒ at Marta's house

11 Which word does NOT belong in the list?

Ⓐ library
Ⓑ classroom
Ⓒ living room

9 Where did Marta live before she moved?

Ⓐ Florida
Ⓑ Ohio
Ⓒ Texas

GO ON ▶

Short passage (Nonfiction)

Teacher Read-Aloud

Listen to the article "All Kinds of Weather." Then answer Numbers 12 through 16.

All Kinds of Weather

Take a look outside. What is the weather like? Is the sun shining or hiding? Are there clouds in the sky? Maybe it is raining or snowing. There are many kinds of weather.

Warm, sunny days are very nice. Children can go outside to play. People can swim or fish in the lake. Plants like sunshine, too. The sun helps them make food so they can grow.

Is it a cloudy day? Clouds are made up of tiny drops of water. Sometimes the clouds look like soft, white pillows.

Other times they are thin and low. Clouds can bring rain or snow. The wind pushes clouds across the sky.

Step outside and look up into the sky. It could be sunny or windy or cloudy. Every day can bring a different kind of weather.

GO ON ▶

12

What is the article mostly about?

Ⓐ There are many different kinds of weather.

Ⓑ It is fun to play outside on warm, sunny days.

Ⓒ Winds from thunderstorms can be strong.

13

Kites and toy sailboats move best on what type of days?

Ⓐ windy days

Ⓑ rainy days

Ⓒ cloudy days

14

Which is a fact from this article?

Ⓐ People always swim outside on cold days.

Ⓑ White clouds are giant cotton balls.

Ⓒ Strong winds usually blow during stormy weather.

15

What pushes clouds across the sky?

Ⓐ wind

Ⓑ the sun

Ⓒ rain

GO ON ▶

Name _____ Date _____

Write/Draw

16

> Draw a picture of your favorite kind of weather, and explain why it is your favorite.

STOP

ISAT Test Practice
© Harcourt • Grade 1

12

Prompt

What is your favorite animal?

Draw a picture and write about your favorite animal.

ISAT Test Practice
© Harcourt • Grade 1

STOP

Short passage (Functional)

Teacher Read-Aloud

Listen to the article "Red or Blue?" Then answer Numbers 1 through 3.

Red or Blue?

Many birds live in North America. One bird is the robin. It has red feathers on its chest. It eats worms and fruit. Robins grow to be about 11 inches long.

Another North American bird is the blue jay. Its feathers are mostly blue. It gathers nuts for food. Blue jays grow to be about 11 inches long, too.

Both birds use their wings to fly. A robin has gray wings. A blue jay's wings are mostly blue. Robins and blue jays fly south in winter.

GO ON ▶

1

How are robins and blue jays the same?

Ⓐ Both eat worms and fruit.

Ⓑ Both have gray wings.

Ⓒ Both fly south in the winter.

2

How are robins different from blue jays?

Ⓐ Robins use their wings to fly.

Ⓑ Robins have red chest feathers.

Ⓒ Robins grow to be 11 inches long.

3

How do these birds move to the south in winter?

Ⓐ They use their wings to fly.

Ⓑ They gather nuts for food.

Ⓒ They follow the moon.

GO ON ▶

Name _____ Date _____

Short passage (Fiction)

Teacher Read-Aloud

Listen to the story "Turtles." Then answer Numbers 4 through 6.

Turtles

Rosa sees a turtle at the zoo. She wants to know what turtles eat. Her mom takes her to the library. There, they find books about animals. Rosa knows that a turtle is an animal. She and her mom look at the books. Rosa sees a book with a turtle on the cover. It is a book about turtles. She takes the book to the librarian and checks it out. Then, Rosa and her mom go home with the book. Rosa is excited to learn more about turtles.

GO ON ▶

4

What do you predict Rosa will do next?

Ⓐ Rosa will buy a turtle at the pet store.

Ⓑ Rosa will feed turtles at the zoo.

Ⓒ Rosa will read the book about turtles.

6

Where did Rosa and her mom find a book about turtles?

Ⓐ at the library

Ⓑ at the zoo

Ⓒ at their home

5

Where did Rosa see a turtle?

Ⓐ in her yard

Ⓑ at the zoo

Ⓒ at her school

GO ON ▶

Short passage (Functional)

Teacher Read-Aloud

Listen to the story "Come and Get It!" Then answer Numbers 7 through 11.

Come and Get It!

By Tess Jones

My dad makes the best pancakes. One day I asked him to show me how to make them.

My dad said, "We'll make the pancakes together on Saturday, Tess."

Saturday came, and we started to make breakfast together. First, I got a big bowl. I cracked three eggs and put them in the bowl. Then, I used a fork to mix the eggs. Next, I put in one cup of milk and mixed again.

Dad put in other things. I mixed everything together with a big spoon. Then, he put a pan on the stove and turned the stove on. Next, Dad helped me carefully put some batter into the hot pan. Finally, he showed me how to flip the pancakes so that they would cook well on both sides.

GO ON ▶

7 To make the pancakes, what did Tess do first?

Ⓐ got a big bowl
Ⓑ put in milk
Ⓒ added eggs

8 Where does this story happen?

Ⓐ at school
Ⓑ in a kitchen
Ⓒ outside

9 What is this story mostly about?

Ⓐ cracking eggs
Ⓑ making pancakes
Ⓒ eating pancakes

10 Why does Tess want her dad to show her how to make pancakes?

Ⓐ She is hungry.
Ⓑ She has never had pancakes before.
Ⓒ He makes the best pancakes.

11 Who wrote this story?

Ⓐ Tess
Ⓑ Tess's dad
Ⓒ Tess's friend

GO ON ▶

Short passage (Nonfiction)

Listen to the article "Is It a Bear?" Then answer Numbers 12 through 16.

Teacher Read-Aloud

Is It a Bear?
by Andy Green

Have you ever seen a koala? The koala looks like a small bear. The animal has soft gray or brown fur and bushy gray ears. Its eyes are shiny black. It has a big, shiny black nose, too. Some people think it looks like a toy bear.

Koalas are not really bears. They belong to the same animal family as the kangaroo. Animals in this family are pouch animals. The mother koala has a <u>pouch</u>, or pocket, in front of her stomach. She carries her baby in this pouch.

A baby koala is tiny when it is born. It is the size of your little finger. This tiny baby is safe inside the mother's pouch. When the baby is about six months old, it is ready to leave the pouch. Then the baby koala rides on its mother's back. The mother carries her baby for another six months. Finally, the baby is ready to be on its own.

GO ON ▶

12

How big is a baby koala?

Ⓐ as big as a squirrel

Ⓑ as big as a baby elephant

Ⓒ as big as your little finger

13

What does the word pouch mean in this article?

Ⓐ fruit

Ⓑ baby

Ⓒ pocket

14

What do both koalas and kangaroos have?

Ⓐ pouches

Ⓑ wings

Ⓒ shiny black noses

15

Which animal does NOT belong?

Ⓐ kangaroo

Ⓑ koala

Ⓒ fish

GO ON ▶

Write/Draw

16

Draw a picture and write about what happens after the baby koala is about six months old.

STOP

Prompt

What is your favorite food?

Draw a picture and write about your favorite food.

ISAT Test Practice
© Harcourt • Grade 1

STOP

Name _____ Date _____

Short passage (Fiction)

Listen to the story "Fun at the Park." Then answer Numbers 1 through 3.

Fun at the Park

Mama takes Daniel to the park. Mama sits on a park bench. Daniel skips over to the playground.

First, Daniel sees a tree. It has big green leaves. He watches a squirrel climb the tree. Daniel wishes he could climb, too. He asks Mama.

"No," says Mama. Daniel may not climb the tree.

Mama watches Daniel go up a slide. He steps on the ladder. At the top, he sits with his legs out front. Then, he goes down. Daniel likes the slide.

A swing set stands next to the slide. Daniel wants to swing. He calls to Mama.

"Will you push me?" asks Daniel.

Mama smiles as she walks over to Daniel.

GO ON ▶

1

What do you predict Mama will do next?

Ⓐ She will catch Daniel from the slide.

Ⓑ She will help Daniel climb the tree.

Ⓒ She will push Daniel on the swing.

2

What did Daniel like at the playground?

Ⓐ a slide

Ⓑ a lake

Ⓒ a restaurant

3

What did Mama do at the park?

Ⓐ she climbed a tree

Ⓑ she sat on a bench

Ⓒ she fed the squirrels

GO ON ▶

Short passage (Fiction)

Teacher Read-Aloud

Listen to the story "Glen's Trip." Then answer Numbers 4 through 6.

Glen's Trip

Glen is going on a trip. He will visit his grandma. She lives far away.

Glen's mom finds his backpack. He puts his clothes in it.

Glen packs his pants first. Then, he packs his shirts. He packs a jacket, too. It might be cold at Grandma's.

Glen's mom asks, "Did you pack your toothbrush?"

He had forgotten his toothbrush! Glen quickly tucks his toothbrush in his bag. He is ready for his trip.

GO ON ▶

4 What does Glen pack last?

Ⓐ his toothbrush
Ⓑ his shirts
Ⓒ his pants

5 Where is Glen going?

Ⓐ on a camping trip
Ⓑ to the city park
Ⓒ to visit his grandma

6 Why did Glen pack a jacket?

Ⓐ He thinks it might get cold.
Ⓑ He wants to have enough to wear.
Ⓒ He wants to fill his backpack.

GO ON ▶

Short passage (Fiction)

Listen to the story "Chipmunk Forgets." Then answer Numbers 7 through 11.

Chipmunk Forgets

Chipmunk was walking in the woods. He was looking for nuts. His basket was almost full. Just then, Owl and Beaver came down the path. They were carrying flowers and a cake.

"Hello, Chipmunk," said Owl. "Are you ready to go to Squirrel's party? I see you have your present."

"Oh, my!" said Chipmunk. "I forgot all about the party. I'm glad I met you!"

"Let's go," said Beaver. "We don't want to be late."

GO ON ▶

7 What did Chipmunk forget?

Ⓐ Squirrel's party

Ⓑ a basket of nuts

Ⓒ where Squirrel lives

8 What do you think Chipmunk will give to Squirrel?

Ⓐ flowers

Ⓑ a cake

Ⓒ nuts

9 How can you tell that Chipmunk is surprised?

Ⓐ He says, "Oh, my!"

Ⓑ He sees his friends.

Ⓒ He is carrying a basket.

10 Where does this story happen?

Ⓐ in the woods

Ⓑ at a party

Ⓒ in Squirrel's house

11 How full was Chipmunk's basket?

Ⓐ empty

Ⓑ almost full

Ⓒ full

GO ON ▶

Short passage (Fiction)

**Listen to the story "A Very Special Drawing."
Then answer Numbers 12 through 17.**

A Very Special Drawing

Paul, Carlos, and Ann decided to have a contest.

"We can have a dog-drawing contest," suggested Ann.

The friends got paper and crayons and started to draw Ann's dog, Dusty. Then they asked Ann's grandpa to be the judge.

"I think each picture looks just like Dusty," Grandpa said. "All three of you are winners!"

The next day Paul and Carlos went to Ann's house. Ann looked sad when she answered the door.

"What's the matter?" they asked.

Ann said, "I can't find Dusty."

"I have an idea," said Carlos. "Let's put our pictures of Dusty in store windows. Someone may see the pictures and know where Dusty is."

Early the next morning, Ann heard a knock on the door. There stood a lady with Dusty.

"You found my dog!" cried Ann.

"Yes," the lady said. "The picture looked just like him."

GO ON ▶

12 What is the story mostly about?

Ⓐ a lost dog
Ⓑ three friends
Ⓒ Grandpa

13 What kind of contest did the children have?

Ⓐ racing
Ⓑ baking
Ⓒ drawing

14 How did Ann feel when she could not find Dusty?

Ⓐ happy
Ⓑ glad
Ⓒ sad

15 What happened after the lady found Dusty?

Ⓐ She took Dusty to Ann.
Ⓑ The children drew more pictures.
Ⓒ Dusty got lost.

16 Which sentence uses the word judge correctly?

Ⓐ She poured judge over her ice cream.
Ⓑ He will judge the pie-eating contest.
Ⓒ We bought a judge of syrup.

GO ON ▶

Write/Draw

17

Grandpa looks at three drawings of Dusty. Draw Grandpa's face as he looks at the drawings. Write how he feels about the drawings.

_____

- -

_____

- -

_____

- -

_____

STOP

Prompt

What do you like to do when it snows?

Draw a picture and write about what you do outside in the snow.

ISAT Test Practice
© Harcourt • Grade 1

STOP

Name _____ Date _____

Short passage (Fiction)

Read the story "Squirrel's Hat." Then answer Numbers 1 through 3.

Squirrel's Hat

Squirrel was worried. He couldn't remember where he put his winter hat. It was getting cold outside. He'd need his hat soon.

"I'm so forgetful," Squirrel said to his friends, Rabbit and Frog.

"We'll help you look for your hat," said Frog.

Rabbit looked under every piece of furniture in Squirrel's house. Frog searched all the closets. Squirrel thought hard about where else his hat could be.

Finally, Rabbit said, "I found it! It was under your bed."

GO ON ▶

1

Who finds Squirrel's missing hat?

Ⓐ Frog

Ⓑ Rabbit

Ⓒ Squirrel

2

Where was Squirrel's hat?

Ⓐ in a closet

Ⓑ under a chair

Ⓒ under the bed

3

Why did Squirrel need a hat?

Ⓐ It was getting cold outside.

Ⓑ He liked wearing his winter hat.

Ⓒ Rabbit and Frog took his.

GO ON ▶

Short passage (Nonfiction)

Read the article "Animal Nests." Then answer Numbers 4 through 6.

Animal Nests

Some birds make their homes in the treetops. Birds' homes are called nests. The birds find the best branch. Then they gather twigs, leaves, and weeds. A bird's nest is shaped like a cup. Mud helps the nest keep its shape. This is a snug home for birds.

Rabbits make homes on the land. A mother rabbit makes her nest in tall weeds. She makes a flat spot in the weeds. Then she adds some of her fur to make the nest soft.

GO ON ▶

4

Why did the author write "Animal Nests"?

Ⓐ To tell an entertaining story about a bird

Ⓑ To tell how to take care of a rabbit

Ⓒ To inform about bird and rabbit nests

5

A bird's nest is built in the shape of —

Ⓐ a plate

Ⓑ a cup

Ⓒ a treetop

6

Why does the mother rabbit add some of her fur to the nest?

Ⓐ to make the nest larger

Ⓑ to keep the nest flat

Ⓒ to make the nest soft

GO ON ▶

Poetry

Read the poem "Jumping Jack." Then answer Numbers 7 through 9.

Jumping Jack

Bump! Thump! Clump!

There goes Jack,

Who likes to jump.

He races and chases.

He zooms all around.

In big and small spaces,

He turns upside down.

It's easy to tell

Just how Jack feels,

By how many times

He does his cartwheels.

Happy or sad,

Or even just sore,

That old Jumping Jack

Will jump up some more!

GO ON ▶

7

What does the poem
tell about Jack?

Ⓐ Jack is in first grade.

Ⓑ Jack likes to jump
around.

Ⓒ Jack is having a
birthday party

8

Where does Jack do
cartwheels?

Ⓐ in big and small
spaces

Ⓑ in his classroom

Ⓒ at the doctor's office

9

Why did the author
write the poem
"Jumping Jack"?

Ⓐ to tell how to do a
cartwheel

Ⓑ to teach a lesson
about showing
feelings

Ⓒ to tell a story about
a boy who jumps

GO ON ▶

Short passage (Fiction)

Read the story "Duck Food." Then answer Numbers 10 through 15.

Duck Food

Bill and Dave walk in the park. They stop to watch the ducks on the lake. The ducks swim toward the boys. The ducks quack loudly.

"The ducks want food," says Dave. The boys reach into their pockets. They have marbles, lint, string, and rocks. They don't have anything they can feed the ducks.

Then Dave shouts, "Look, I found five dollars!" He picks up the money and looks around the park. He does not see anyone who might have lost the money.

"I have an idea," Dave says.

The boys go away from the park. They come back later. Each boy has a bag of bread. They walk to the lake. The ducks swim toward the boys. The boys begin to feed the ducks little bits of bread.

GO ON ▶

10

Where does this story take place?

Ⓐ in a zoo

Ⓑ in a park

Ⓒ in a school

11

What do the boys NOT have in their pockets?

Ⓐ duck food

Ⓑ string

Ⓒ rocks

12

What does Dave do with the money?

Ⓐ He buys bread.

Ⓑ He gives the money to the ducks.

Ⓒ He loses the money.

13

What happens at the end of the story?

Ⓐ The boys find money.

Ⓑ The boys feed the ducks.

Ⓒ The boys buy bread.

14

Look at the picture. How many ducks are there?

Ⓐ 5

Ⓑ 6

Ⓒ 7

GO ON ▶

Name _____ Date _____

Extended Response

15

How do you think the boys feel about feeding the ducks? Why do you think this?

_____

- -

_____

_____

- -

_____

- -

_____

_____

- -

_____

_____

- -

_____

- -

_____

_____

- -

_____

_____

- -

_____

STOP

ISAT Test Practice
© Harcourt • Grade 1

Prompt

Who are some people in your family? Draw and write about
one or two people in your family.

STOP

Short passage (Fiction)

Read the story "Albert's New House." Then answer Numbers 1 through 3.

Albert's New House

Each day Albert goes with his mom or dad to see their new house. Soon they will move to their new house. Albert has waited a long time to move!

Albert liked his new house. It had a big backyard.

Albert helped his mom and dad pick paint for the walls. The kitchen will be yellow. The bathroom will be red.

One day, Albert and his dad went to the store. "Let's pick one more color," said Dad. "This time it is for your room."

Albert chose green paint. "My room will be the best!" Albert said.

GO ON ▶

1

What is this story mostly about?

Ⓐ where Albert lives

Ⓑ the color of the new house

Ⓒ Albert and his family are moving

3

Why did Albert like his new house?

Ⓐ it had a big backyard

Ⓑ the house was painted green

Ⓒ he had waited a long time to move

2

Why did Albert go to the store with his dad?

Ⓐ to see their new house

Ⓑ to choose a paint color for his room

Ⓒ to help his dad carry some paint

GO ON ▶

Short passage (Fiction)

Read the story "The Math Page." Then answer Numbers 4 through 6.

The Math Page

It was almost time for school. Jerome waited outside. He got out his page of math problems from his backpack. He had spent a long time on his math last night. He wanted it to be perfect.

Just then, a strong breeze came. The breeze swept the page from Jerome's hands. His math problems were blowing away! Jerome ran to catch the page. He did not catch it. He was very sad.

Later, it was time to show the math problems to his teacher. Jerome was upset. He did not have his math page.

Then his teacher said, "Jerome, here is your math page. I found it outside." Jerome smiled. He was happy. His math problems were perfect.

GO ON ▶

4

What happened to make Jerome upset?

Ⓐ Jerome lost his math problems.

Ⓑ Jerome missed the school bus.

Ⓒ Jerome was outside before school.

6

Where did Jerome's teacher find the math page?

Ⓐ in Jerome's backpack

Ⓑ outside in the yard

Ⓒ on the school bus

5

What happened to Jerome's math page?

Ⓐ Jerome did not finish it.

Ⓑ Jerome left it in the house.

Ⓒ The wind swept the page away.

GO ON ▶

Short passage (Fiction)

Read the story "Party Time." Then answer Numbers 7 through 10.

Party Time

Maggie was excited. Her family was having a party. There was so much to do! Maggie helped get ready for the party.

First, she helped her dad clean. Maggie put away her books and clothes. She made her bed. Then she dusted the tabletops.

Next, she helped her mom shop for food. They went to the bakery. Maggie chose muffins for the party. The bakery smelled so good. The smells made her very hungry!

Last, Maggie got dressed. She put on her best shirt and pants.

Maggie's dad said, "Thank you for helping me clean, Maggie."

Maggie's mom said, "Thank you for helping me shop, Maggie. The muffins taste great!"

Everyone had a great time at the party.

Maggie had the best time of all!

GO ON ▶

7

What happened to make Maggie hungry?

Ⓐ Dad thanked Maggie for helping.

Ⓑ Maggie put on her best shirt.

Ⓒ The bakery smelled good.

8

What does Maggie do after she goes to the bakery?

Ⓐ Maggie gets dressed for the party.

Ⓑ Maggie makes her bed.

Ⓒ Maggie dusts the tabletops.

9

How did Maggie help her dad?

Ⓐ She went to get some muffins.

Ⓑ She put away her clothes.

Ⓒ She got dressed for the party.

10

What happens at the end of the story?

Ⓐ Maggie puts away her books and clothes.

Ⓑ Everyone has a great time at the party.

Ⓒ Mom says that the muffins are great.

GO ON ▶

ISAT Test Practice
© Harcourt • Grade 1

Name _____   Date _____

Short passage (Functional)

Read the article "Clean Hands." Then answer Numbers 11 through 15.

Clean Hands

Your hands may look clean. But they might just be dirty.

We all have germs on our hands. Germs are too small to see. They can make you sick. That is why you need to scrub your hands. Washing your hands gets rid of some germs.

Wash your hands every day. Wash before you eat, and after using the bathroom. Wash after petting animals or playing outside. Wash after blowing your nose or sneezing.

Follow these steps to wash some germs off your hands.

Hand Washing Steps

Step 1	Wet your hands in warm water.
Step 2	Use soap. Rub your hands to make the soap foamy.
Step 3	Rub between your fingers. Clean under your nails.
Step 4	Use warm water to wash off the soap.
Step 5	Dry your hands with a clean cloth.

GO ON ▶

11

What is the main idea
of "Clean Hands"?

Ⓐ Everyone eats and
plays outside.

Ⓑ Germs are easy to
see on your hands.

Ⓒ Wash your hands to
get rid of germs.

12

Read this sentence
from the article.
    That is why you need
    to scrub your hands.
What does the word
scrub mean?

Ⓐ clap

Ⓑ clean

Ⓒ wave

13

How are your hands
different after you wash
them?

Ⓐ Some germs are gone.

Ⓑ Your hands are cold.

Ⓒ The nails will grow.

14

What is the last step on
the chart?

Ⓐ Rub your hands

Ⓑ Dry your hands

Ⓒ Clean your nails

GO ON ▶

ISAT Test Practice
© Harcourt • Grade 1

Name _____ Date _____

Extended Response

15

Explain what the chart on page 51 tells you about washing your hands.

_____

- -

_____

_____

- -

_____

_____

- -

_____

_____

- -

_____

_____

- -

_____

_____

- -

_____

_____

- -

_____

STOP

Prompt

What is your favorite season?

Write and draw about something you like to do in your favorite season.

GO ON ▶